THE SPACE STOWAWAY

a novel by Malorie Blackman

CONTENTS

D0233693

CHAPTER 1: SAM ARRIVES

Josh sat down at the console and sighed deeply.
Yet another deserted planet. No sign of life
anywhere. Just scrubland and desert, stretching
on for mile after mile after mile.

"Let's take off. There's nothing here."
Josh's hands clenched into frustrated fists. He
watched miserably out of the view screen as his
ship lifted off the surface of the planet. With
each moment, the ground below him got further
and further away.

"Escaping this planet's orbit in seven seconds ... six ... five ..."

Josh braced himself.

"Three ... two ..." The computer's toneless voice counted down relentlessly.

Josh was thrown from side to side in his chair as his ship escaped the planet's gravitational pull. Minutes passed as Josh watched the planet. He waited until it was no more than the size of a football behind him, before he spoke again.

"Daily log. Transmission start." Josh spoke wearily to his computer. "This is the continuing log of the Starship *Gayl.* Joshua Doyle reporting. This is my five hundred and thirty-first day alone in this ... this metal box. I've taken off from yet another planet with no animal life on it."

Josh stood up and walked towards the view screen. The planet he'd just left was now fingernail sized. He watched it without blinking, trying to hold on to it in his mind for as long as possible. He'd hoped so hard that this time, *this time* he'd find someone ...

"I have no way of knowing how much of this is being recorded, so every day I force myself to record the story of what happened to the rest of the crew – just in case all my other transmissions didn't work properly, or the records are lost. I have no way of being sure."

Josh paused, asking himself why he bothered to go through this day after day after day. It was pointless – and yet here he was again.

"I keep recording these messages because ... because even if I don't get home alive, maybe these transmissions will still be of use to someone – if this ship is eventually found." Josh returned to his chair and sat back.

"The rest of the crew were wiped out by a mystery plague after we left Jelphar-8." Josh swallowed hard and forced himself to carry on. "This plague drove the crew totally crazy before they all died. They would rave about being shadowed, about 'separating'. They all seemed to hallucinate about similar things.

"Some of the crew became destructive, trying to smash anything or anyone in their way. That's why the navigation system is flaky. It got bashed by Lieutenant Price, the first officer. He kept saying that the computer was trying to eat his belly button. I repaired what I could but I couldn't fix up the library link, so there's no way to patch the navigational system into the library files for the star charts. If the star charts weren't already in the navigational system's computer memory, then I would have had to plot the ship's course manually – and navigating isn't exactly my strong point.

"Which is why I haven't a clue where we are!

"And that's the reason why I don't know if this transmission is even being recorded properly. The ship's logs are stored in the library. I'm hoping everything I say is being kept somewhere in the main memory core until the link between it and the library systems can be repaired. But I don't know.

"I also don't have a clue why I was the only one to survive the plague. Not being a biologist or even into biology, I doubt if I'm ever going to find out either! But every day I peer into the microscope, studying blood samples, comparing my blood to that of some of the dead crew, hoping that something will leap out at me."

Day in, day out, Josh made the same report.

Give up ... a voice inside him urged. *It's hopeless. What's the point? Give up* ...

Josh had made a real effort to concentrate on what he was doing – to not listen to the voices in his head.

"My mum was captain of this ship – Captain Trisha Doyle. She died with the rest of the crew. I wish ... I sometimes wish I'd died with everyone else."

It was a wish Josh had made more and more frequently lately.

"I hate being alone ..."

"Er, sorry! But you're not alone! Not any more!'"

Josh leapt out of his chair like a scalded cat. He stared at the boy standing in the doorway. A boy of about his age, twelve or thirteen, with jet black hair and eyes which were just as dark. The boy smiled at him with a mixture of amusement and relief.

"Hi! I'm Sam. Don't call me Samuel. I hate that!" The boy's grin widened.

"Where ... where ... ?"

"From the planet you've just left. I'm a stowaway!" Sam laughed. "I reckoned that by now we'd be too far away from the planet for you to turn back."

"But I searched the planet surface. I searched for miles."

Josh still couldn't believe it. There was actually someone else on the bridge talking to him. A real, live person and not just the toneless, flat computer voice he'd had to put up with for almost *two years.*

"I know. I hid and watched you."

"Why didn't you come up to me? Why didn't you say something?"

"I wanted to get off the planet."

"I would have taken you off," Josh replied, confused.

"I didn't know that – and I couldn't take the chance of you leaving me behind," Sam shrugged.

Josh and Sam watched each other for a few moments in silence. Josh's mind was buzzing. He wasn't going to be alone any more. Someone else was on the ship. But that very fact made him cautious. What kind of boy was Sam? How had he managed to hide himself on the planet? Was he telling the truth? Maybe he was an alien in disguise ... Shapeshifters were meant to be quite common in this sector of the galaxy.

"How did you come to be on the planet in the first place?" Josh asked at last.

"I stowed away on a freighter a while ago. When they landed on that last planet, they found me and threw me off their ship," Sam replied.

"Why did you stow away on the freighter?"

"That's obvious, isn't it? I didn't have the credits to pay for the journey. And I needed to get home – or as close as I could to it."

"And where's home?"

"Earth originally, but at the moment I'd settle for anywhere away from here!" Sam smiled.

"*Earth?* I'm from Earth. That's where I'm trying to get back to," Josh exclaimed.

"Great! Then you can give me a ride all the way home," said Sam.

"How long were you on that planet we just left?" asked Josh.

"Just over a month, maybe more."

"How did you live? What did you live on?"

Josh had found only a few plants and precious little water on the surface when he'd gone out scouting.

"D'you mind if we leave the questions until later?" Sam asked. "Right now, all I want to do is stuff my face and sleep. I'm exhausted."

"Yeah ... Yeah, all right," Josh said reluctantly. "I'll show you to a room – you've got two hundred and ninety-nine to choose from."

"I heard part of your log when I came in," Sam said. "So the rest of the crew are all dead?"

Josh nodded slowly.

"It's just you?"

"It's just me," Josh agreed.

"Not any more." Sam shook his head. "Now it's both of us."

Something in the way Sam said that made Josh really, *really* worried.

CHAPTER 2: SUSPICIOUS

The first thing Josh did, once he'd shown Sam to his room and explained how to use the food generator, was to go down to the Engineering section of the ship. He wanted to check his sci-cameras. The sci-cameras had informed him that there was no sign of life on the last planet he'd visited. But Sam had arrived ...

There had to be something drastically wrong with the equipment.

Josh spent over an hour running test after test on the sci-cameras but he couldn't find a single malfunction. They appeared to be working just fine. So where had Sam sprung from?

Defeated, and more than a little confused, Josh returned to the bridge.

"Daily log. Transmission resume."

Josh took one last look around to make sure he was completely alone before he said, "I've picked up a passenger from the last planet I landed on. He says his name is Sam. He says he was dumped on the planet and all he wants to do is return home to Earth ..."

Josh frowned deeply. Sam was the first breathing, talking, living creature he'd seen since the rest of the crew of the *Gayl* had died of the mystery plague. And Sam wasn't just any old life form, he was a boy like Josh. Josh knew he should be feeling ecstatic. But all he felt was uneasy, wary. Sam had arrived with too many unanswered questions.

"I don't know about Sam," Josh continued with his transmission. "But I intend to keep my eyes on him and watch my back. There's something about ..."

"How long will it take us to reach Earth?" Josh spun round in his chair.

"I thought you were going to get some sleep?" Josh said, wondering how much Sam had heard of what he'd just said.

"Couldn't sleep. Too excited!" Sam smiled. "You must be really smart, to fly this ship all by yourself."

"Transmission halt," Josh told his computer.

As Josh watched, Sam wandered over to the tactical console and examined the controls.

"You know how to operate all of this, do you?" Sam asked, ready to be impressed.

"I know how most of the bridge functions work, but it's still a lot to do by myself – even with the computer's help," Josh said.

"I won't be much use to you, I'm afraid," Sam shrugged. "I can work a tactical station and the environmental station and that's about it. I never learnt all that really high-tech stuff."

"I'll teach you. Anyway, I only learnt it because my mum was the captain," Josh explained. "And I wanted to be like her – a captain of a starship one day. Not a freighter or a tiddly conveyor ship but a huge starship with a crew of hundreds."

"Doing all this by yourself will make the training back on Earth a doddle," said Sam.

"If we ever get back to Earth," Josh said quietly.

"What d'you mean?" Sam frowned. He moved to sit in the command chair by the second navigational console.

"I mean that maybe you stowed away on the wrong ship," Josh replied. "This ship is badly damaged and most of the systems are either not working as they should or not working at all."

"So what *is* working properly?" Sam asked.

"The autopiloting system still works at a very basic level, except that I have to manually manoeuvre and land the ship myself. The part of the navigation panel that automatically controls landing and take-off is defunct and I have no way of fixing it."

"How many planets have you landed on so far?" Sam asked with concern.

"Nine. Ten, including the last one."

"Oh, that's all right then." Sam relaxed back into his chair. "You obviously know what you're doing."

"Thanks!" Josh said dryly.

"Was there no life on any of those planets?" Sam asked.

Josh shrugged. "No sign of intelligent life – at least, not that I found. In fact I didn't find any animal life of any kind on those planets, just plants, plants, plants! I don't know where I am. I've got no idea which solar system we're currently whirling through. And I've got no idea how far away from Earth we are – or even if we're travelling in the right direction to get to it. Welcome aboard!"

"Well, don't give up." Sam grinned. "You never know, we might wake up one morning and see the Earth right in front of us."

"Hmm." Josh remained non-committal. He'd spent too many days and weeks and months wishing and wistfully daydreaming, and rushing hopefully to his portscreen as soon as he woke up, to start again now.

"What about you?" Josh asked. "I still don't know anything about you. Where are your parents? Where are you stationed? Have you got any brothers and sisters?"

"I'll answer your questions some other time. I think I'll get some sleep now." Sam was out of his chair and off the bridge before Josh could say another word.

Josh waited until the turbo lift doors closed before he turned back to his console.

"Transmission resume. Well, that was Sam," he said. "I can't make him out at all. He says all he wants to do is get back to Earth like me, but he's strange. There's something about him that I don't quite trust. I think I'd better start sleeping with my mum's S-gun under my pillow. I haven't had to do that since the crew went nuts, and I hated doing it. I woke up each morning with a crick in my neck and a splitting headache, but better safe than dead. Transmission end."

CHAPTER 3: A DECISION IS MADE

"Sam! Sam, wake up!" Josh came rushing into Sam's room.

"What ... what is it?" Sam said sleepily, before rolling over and going back to sleep.

They'd been together now for over three months. Josh still wasn't sure about Sam. His constant cheerfulness did get a bit wearing, but he was good company and made Josh laugh. But Sam had a strange habit of disappearing. An hour here, half a day there. Once he'd been missing for three whole days, and he'd refused point-blank to say where he was, in spite of Josh raging at him when he reappeared.

Impatiently Josh shook Sam awake.

"Sam, there's a planet on the view screen. A habitable planet."

Sam's eyes flew open. "A planet? Really? Is it Earth?" he asked hopefully.

Josh shook his head. "We're not in that solar system. But it's a very similar planet. The atmosphere's oxygen and nitrogen, with a few trace elements – and get this! The main sci-camera has picked up signs of animal life on the planet. The signals are very strange, they keep appearing and disappearing, but they're definitely present. Something's active down there."

"Friend or foe?"

"Now how in the galaxy would I know that until I've met them?" Josh asked. "I still haven't made up my mind about *you*, and we've been stuck together for months now!"

"Very funny," Sam said.

Josh started laughing at the unamused look on Sam's face. Sam pushed Josh aside, before getting out of his rest cubicle. They both raced for the bridge.

Josh looked at the view screen before studying the scanners and the main sci-camera's findings. He still didn't know where they were. It could have been any one of fifty planets indicated by the navigational system's computer memory – and that excluded all the solar system details held in the library files which were no longer linked to the main computer. Josh turned to look back at the planet.

The deep emptiness within him regretted that it wasn't Earth. It wasn't home. But it was habitable. And if there was life on the planet, maybe he could just land and settle there. It was better than living in a metal box of a spaceship for the rest of his life.

"Sam, if the people down there are friendly, what do you say to just staying put once we land on this planet?" Josh asked.

Sam looked at him speculatively.

"Is that what you want to do?"

Josh shrugged. "I don't know. This might be the last habitable planet we see before our engines burn themselves out through lack of maintenance. On the other hand, the very next solar system we stumble across might be ours. So what do we do?"

"You have to make this decision," Sam said, turning his head to look through the view screen again.

Josh frowned at Sam's profile. Sam's brown-black eyes were clear and sharp, but his lips were now turned downwards in a deep frown.

"What are you thinking?" Josh asked curiously.

"I'm wondering what you'll decide." Sam replied.

"You have some input into this too," Josh pointed out. "If I stay, so do you. Or are you thinking of taking the *Gayl* if I stay put, and carrying on without me?"

"I can't do that." Sam shrugged. "I have no idea how to fly this bucket by myself."

"I could teach you." Josh said.

"Why?" Sam frowned suspiciously.

"Why not?"

"So you finally trust me, do you?" Sam laughed. "You don't think I'm some sort of alien just waiting for the right moment to gobble you up or something?"

"Don't be so stupid!" Josh snapped, annoyed because that thought *had* crossed his mind when he'd first met Sam – along with several other thoughts of a similar nature.

Sam and Josh watched out of the view screen.

"Don't you believe you'll ever see Earth again?" Sam asked.

"I don't know. But I'm wondering what happens if we don't get back to Earth. I don't want to spend the rest of my days spinning in this tub."

"So you want us to stay?"

"What do you think?"

"Oh no you don't, Josh. You're the captain of this crate. Well, the captain's son at any rate. The decision is yours and yours alone. I'm just an uninvited guest – remember?" Sam said.

"In that case ... in that case, we'll land on that planet and see what's down there," Josh decided. "And if its friendly, we'll stay."

"I hope you know what you are doing." Sam said.

Josh shook his head. "That's just the trouble," he replied. "I haven't got a *clue* what I'm doing."

CHAPTER 4: A CLOSE CALL

"Hang on, Sam, this is going to be a bumpy landing."

Josh applied the retro-thrusters. The ship jerked and shuddered before it hit the ground. Josh and Sam were thrown violently forwards then backwards. Josh unbuckled his safety strap once the ship had stopped moving. He moved over to the control console to run an error check on the landing gear.

"Oh no! I don't believe it," Josh exclaimed with dismay.

"What is it?" Sam joined him at the control console, scrutinizing the instrument panel.

Every part of Josh's body slumped. His heart sank down to his toenails.

"The retro-thrusters have disengaged." Josh breathed deeply, trying to control the sense of despair threatening to overwhelm him. "That's it, then. There's no way we can attempt another landing now."

"Can you fix it?" Sam asked.

"No way. It's a Corporation Spaceport job. We don't have a hope of fixing it here, even if we did have the proper equipment – which we don't. I just don't have that expertise."

"So what do we do now?"

"I'd say our decision has been forced on us." Josh replied. "This is it. This is the last planet we can safely land on. Either we stay here or we take off again and drift, hoping to be pulled to safety by a full-force tractor beam. There's no way I can risk another planetary landing."

"What you're saying is, even if we did stumble across Earth, we'd have no way of landing on the planet surface," Sam realized.

Josh nodded. "That's it in a nutshell. I think we're destined never to see home again."

"We're not beaten yet," Sam said grimly.

Josh looked at him. He smiled suddenly. "Down but not out, right, Sam?"

Sam smiled back. "What we need to do now is find out what sort of planet we've landed on. Maybe we *could* make this our home."

"We'd better put on our environmental suits and check it out," said Josh.

"There's no need. Our instruments show that this planet's atmosphere is very much like our own on Earth," Sam said.

"And you trust our instruments to be not just undamaged but correct?" Josh raised his eyebrows.

"Yes, I'm sure they are all right," Sam nodded.

"Sure enough to stake your life on it?"

Sam didn't reply.

"Tell me more about the life forms on this planet," he said at last.

"The computer says there's lots of different types of life down there. We'd have to leave the ship to make a closer study, but I think ..."

Josh never had a chance to finish his sentence. At that moment, the ground began to vibrate violently. The ship lurched, throwing both Josh and Sam across the bridge.

"What ... what is it? An earthquake?" Josh asked, grabbing hold of the navigational control console as he stared out of the view screen.

The purple and pale yellow flora all around was bending and shaking as if in the grip of a vast gale. A deafening roar echoed through the ship and once again the ship rocked.

Josh fought his way across to the control console. Frantically he viewed the panel, punching in data of his own as he tried to assess just what was going on outside. Another jolt of the *Gayl* flung Josh backwards. He grimaced as his elbows cracked against the hard bridge floor.

"It's not an earthquake. At least, not as we know it." Josh shook his head. "According to the computer there is no sign of an earthquake in this area."

"Then what is it?" Sam made for the control console.

"The ground vibrations seem to be caused by something ... something colossal moving quickly in this direction."

"I ... I don't like this," Josh said slowly.

He looked out of the view screen. There was nothing but vegetation to be seen, but the terrible roar was growing louder.

"Maybe we'd see what was going on better from the air?" Sam said.

"Are we running away?"

"Whilst we've still got the chance – yes!" Sam replied quickly.

"You said it!" Josh agreed, relieved. "Brace in!"

Josh and Sam fell into the command seats. Josh activated his body brace to guard against any impact on the ship until they reached orbit.

"On my mark ... three, two, one, mark," Josh said, keying in the lift-off sequence.

The engines roared into life. Josh and Sam felt the force push them hard back into their seats.

"Aargh! Look at that!" Sam pointed to the view screen.

Josh stared in horror. There, crashing through the undergrowth, was the most terrifying thing he'd ever seen. It was huge. It had four antennae with round, grey eyes at the end of each stalk. Its bluish head seemed to be all mouth with two protruding teeth and it had a long, slithering body, the back of which Josh couldn't see because it was so large. The thing moved on many legs, reminding Josh of the centipedes on Earth. Aghast, he realized that the *Gayl* was only slightly larger than one of the thing's eyes. Its tongue flicked out after the *Gayl*.

"Watch out," Sam shouted.

Desperately, Josh hit the tertiary thrust key on the console. The tertiary engines didn't work as well in a planet's atmosphere as they did in space, but they did push the *Gayl* further and faster. The creature's tongue curled below them, just missing the ship. Then, without warning, the creature reared up on to the lower half of its body.

"Fire at it. Do something!" Sam yelled, as the creature began to reach and exceed their altitude.

"I can't fire at it. Not whilst we're taking off," Josh said through gritted teeth.

"We're about to be some alien's lunch if you don't think of something – fast!"

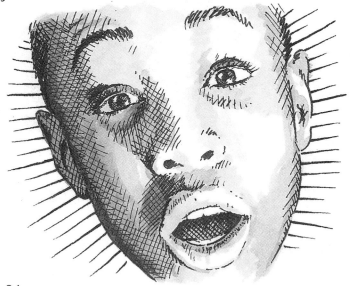

CHAPTER 5: ESCAPE TO NOWHERE

Josh glared at Sam. Quickly he turned back to the control console and started punching in commands with shaky, impatient fingers. A gigantic boom somewhere towards the ship's aft had Josh and Sam rocking violently in their seats. Josh's head was thrown forwards, backwards, forwards until he thought his neck must surely snap.

"What did you do?" Sam asked, rubbing his neck after the *Gayl's* course stabilized.

"I've abandoned the two shuttle craft and I've transferred as much of the *Gayl's* engine heat out-take as possible to the outer skin of the ship."

"But that's what keeps the ship warm," Sam protested.

"I know, so get ready to shiver," Josh said grimly. "I had no choice. It might just make that thing out there think twice about guzzling us.

That's assuming, of course, that I haven't just made us even more appetizing to it!"

"And the shuttle craft? We might need those."

"Tough. Losing those gave us extra lift quickly."

Sam opened his mouth to argue, but one icy glare from Josh and his mouth snapped shut.

"You told me to do something and that's what I did," Josh said. "And we're not out of the woods yet!"

Outside, they grew level with the beast's face. Its tongue flicked and coiled. Its antennae quivered. Josh and Sam both drew back in their chairs.

"Josh ..." Sam said urgently, not taking his eyes off the screen for a single second.

"Keep your fingers crossed," Josh called out. "'Cause here goes!"

The beast's tongue darted out towards the ship. With a gasp of horror, Josh hit two keys on the control console. Immediately, the ship turned sharply right and started falling. Josh felt as if his whole body was being squashed into a ball and pulled into the very chair he sat on. He glanced at Sam. Sam was scowling at him! Josh rekeyed the control console. The ship righted itself and started climbing again.

Out of the view screen, Josh could see the creature's head, its tongue now out of sight above the ship. He hit the forward thrust key again. Now his body was being stretched out, as if on a medieval rack.

"What ... what on earth are you doing?" Sam managed to say. The skin on his face was tightly drawn against his skull.

"Trying to e-escape ..." Josh replied through gritted teeth.

He compensated for the rate they were rising and breathed out with relief when the pressure on the bridge returned to normal.

"Thank goodness for that!" Sam rubbed his sore face.

Josh glowered at him. It would be a close run thing as to which one survived the longest; the ship or his temper. Sam's whingeing was really getting on his nerves.

"I'm using reverse thrust, then forward thrust to escape. If you have any better ideas, be my guest," Josh snapped. "Otherwise, shut up!"

"Josh, do whatever you have to do," Sam said. "I want to survive. That's the only thing I care about."

Sam wrapped his arms around his body. The temperature drop was becoming very uncomfortable, and the roar of the beast outside was deafening.

"Go find your dinner somewhere else," Sam shouted at it.

"Hold on," Josh yelled.

They shot past the creature's head. Its tongue darted out again. The ship jolted as the tongue made contact, but with an even louder howl, the creature withdrew its tongue and fell back down to the ground.

"We did it! We did it!" Sam yelled. "Now turn the heat back on before we freeze to death!"

"You do it." Josh breathed. "I'm ... I'm ...."

Josh could hear his blood roaring in his ears. The bridge was spinning like a gyroscope. Josh forced his hand out across the console and reset the *Gayl*'s heating controls. Immediately the bridge was flooded with warmth. Josh took several deep breaths and slowly the bridge steadied and stopped whirling.

"Are you OK?" Sam asked anxiously.

Josh nodded. "I think so."

They sat in silence for a few moments.

"So what happens now?" Sam asked. For once there was no trace of a smile on his face.

"I don't know."

"We've just escaped to nowhere," Sam said quietly.

"What do you mean?" frowned Josh.

"Take a look at the ship's structural readout," said Sam.

Josh looked down at the data screen on his console and began to read. A few seconds passed before he saw what Sam meant.

"That's it, then." Josh slumped back in his chair. "We don't stand a chance now. Our retro-thrusters have gone and all that turbulence just now has damaged the ship's hull."

"Is it really that bad?" asked Sam.

"Sam, we can't land, and if a tractor beam tries to latch on to us, it'll shake the ship apart," Josh replied grimly.

"Apart from that, it's been quite a good day so far," Sam shrugged.

Josh stared at him. "How can you joke about it? Do you know of any giant marsh-mallows floating about in the galaxy? Because that's about the only thing we can land on."

"Couldn't we land on water?" asked Sam hopefully.

"No. The impact would smash us up. Without the retro-thrusters I wouldn't be able to control our speed before we hit the water," Josh replied. "Any more bright ideas?"

"We're not dead yet," Sam said. "If you want to give up, then go ahead – but I'm not going to."

Josh struggled to find something to say. "Our only option now is to drift until we get picked up." Josh shrugged, desperately trying to hide the fear that churned his stomach. He remembered his mum and the bridge officers and his friends on the *Gayl*. They were all gone. There was only him ... and Sam. What would he do if Sam wasn't there? Giving up would be so easy. It was going on that took courage. Josh bent his head. He didn't want Sam to see how afraid he was.

"Josh, we'll be OK," Sam said uncertainly.

Josh looked at Sam. Their expressions mirrored each other. Startled, Josh realized that for all his blustering and big talk, Sam was just as terrified as he was.

"Fancy a game of cards?" Sam asked at last.

Josh stared. He couldn't believe his ears. But the wry look on Sam's face confirmed it. Josh couldn't help it. He burst out laughing. Cards? At a time like this? Why not?

CHAPTER 6: TORN APART

"Josh! Wake up! Earth! *Earth!*"

Josh opened his eyes. "Don't talk wet," he said crossly. "It's a bit early for one of your jokes, Sam."

"I'm not joking. Look!" Sam pointed to the portscreen.

Something about the expression on Sam's face had Josh springing out of bed and rushing to the portscreen. There, out of the window – Earth! The shape of its continents and shine of its blue oceans was unmistakable.

Josh gasped at the sight of it. He'd forgotten how truly beautiful it was.

"Earth! Home!" Sam and Josh bounded around Josh's bedroom, leaping up and down and whooping wildly.

"We're home ..."

"We did it!"

"We made it!"

"Yesss!"

"Come on! Let's get going." Josh ran out of the room.

"How are we going to land? The retro-thrusters are knackered," Sam puffed, running down the corridor after Josh.

"We'll have to try and get in touch with Space Station Chakawata or Space Station Lessing," Josh answered. "They'll know what to do. They'll probably send someone over to repair enough systems for us to land."

Moments later they were both sitting at their command stations on the bridge.

"I can't believe, after over two years, we've finally made it." Josh's head was swimming. He thought his heart would burst with joy at any moment. If only his mum and the rest of the crew could have been here ... Josh forced the thought out of his head. His mum would have been happy to see him reach home at long last. So *he* should be happy. *He'd done it!*

Josh and Sam grinned at each other, before Josh tried to open a communication channel to the nearest space station.

"This is the Starship *Gayl*, trying to contact Earth. This is the Starship *Gayl*. Please reply." Josh spoke slowly and clearly.

Hissing and crackling sounds filled the communication channel.

"Why aren't they answering?" asked Sam, a worried edge to his voice.

Josh frowned. "This is the Starship *Gayl*, contacting Earth. Are you receiving us?"

"This ..." *Crackle!* "... Lessing. We ..." *Hiss!* "... identify yours ..."

"This is the Starship *Gayl* ..." Josh shouted.

"This is hopeless, is what this is!" Sam sniffed.

"You're not helping," Josh said, annoyed.

"What d'you want me to do?" asked Sam.

" ... Pull ... tractor beam and ..." *Crackle! Crackle! Hiss!* "Stand by!"

Josh and Sam exchanged a horrified look. The space station was going to use its tractor beam to pull the *Gayl* in.

"NO!" Josh yelled frantically. "DON'T USE YOUR TRACTOR BEAM. YOU'LL TEAR US APART."

The *Gayl* gave a severe jolt, almost throwing Josh and Sam out of their chairs.

"Brace in!" Josh told Sam.

They both locked themselves into their seats.

"Warning! The hull structure will be breached in twenty-three seconds ..." the computer cautioned neutrally.

Josh cut the *Gayl*'s engines, but he had to keep his hand on the console to make sure that the autopilot didn't automatically switch them back on again. Under normal circumstances Josh could have overidden the autopilot, but since their narrow escape from the giant centipede, that control on his console no longer worked.

"How far are we away from the space station?" Sam asked.

"At least fifty-five seconds," Josh replied. "We're not going to make it."

"We might last the extra seconds," Sam protested.

"Warning! The hull structure will be breached in fifteen seconds ..."

"The moment the hull's skin is damaged, the first thing that will happen is all the air in the ship will be sucked out into space, taking us right along with it," Josh said.

"If we brace in tight, will the rest of the ship stay together until the space station has us?" Sam asked.

"I don't know," Josh said, adding with a wry smile, "I've never done this before."

"I thought I was the one who made the jokes on this ship!" Sam said.

"Warning! The hull structure will be breached in ten seconds ..."

"Brace right down, Josh. This is going to be rough," said Sam, reinforcing his own seat brace across his chest and legs.

"It won't make any difference. I'm having to constantly override the autopilot to keep the engine off. Once the air is gone, we're both going to pass out," said Josh, grimly. "Then the engines will come back online and we'll smash straight into the space station. And I've no way of warning them."

"Warning! The hull structure will be breached in five seconds ..."

"*I'll* stay awake somehow. I'll do it," Sam said firmly.

"And just how are you going to do that?"
"Two ... One ..."

There was a colossal jolt, followed by what felt to Josh like a kick in his stomach. The air rushed out of his lungs. He shifted the brace around his chest in an effort to breathe. But he couldn't.

The bridge began to whirl around and around. Josh fought to turn his head and look at Sam. Sam looked as if he was in just as much pain as Josh. He slumped across the console. Then the whole world went out like a candle.

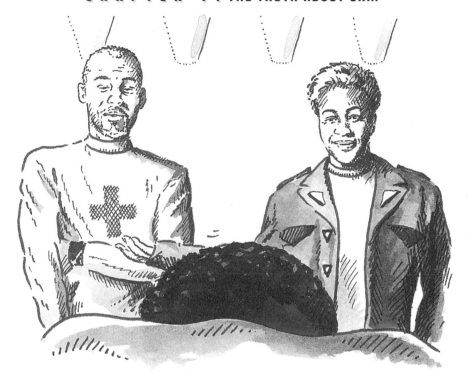

Josh's eyelids fluttered open. It took a few seconds for him to focus. A woman and man stood on either side of his bed. And it was a proper bed. So this couldn't be the *Gayl*! The *Gayl*'s quarters contained rest cubicles, not proper beds. Josh looked up again at the man and the woman. The man was old – in his fifties at least. The woman, in a general's uniform, looked like she was at the good end of her forties.

"Where am I?"

"You're on Space Station Lessing, orbiting Earth," the man replied.

Josh sat up immediately. "Earth? I'm home?"

The woman smiled. "Almost. I'm General Collins. This is Dr Dalder."

Josh nodded impatiently. "Am I really so close to Earth? I'm not just dreaming again?"

"You're home. Look outside."

Josh glanced out of the portscreen. There, vivid and wonderful, was Earth. He'd never get tired of seeing it – ever.

"I've watched all the transmission logs you recorded aboard your ship," said the general. "I'm very sorry about the crew, and your mother. She was a fine officer and my dear friend."

"You knew my mother?" Josh asked. "You were friends with my mother?"

General Collins nodded, then smiled. In that moment, Josh knew the general was his friend as well. He turned back to look at the Earth, unwilling to take his eyes off it for any length of time after so many months spent dreaming about it. He could still hardly believe it. *Earth* ...

"What happened to the *Gayl?*" Josh asked, his eyes still on the portscreen.

"You tell us," General Collins said lightly.

"Your tractor beam ..." Josh suddenly remembered. "I thought you were going to rip our ship apart. I must've blanked out. How long have I been here?" He looked around. "Where's Sam?" Josh knew that his words made little sense but he didn't care about that. They'd done it! Sam had done it. Somehow he'd kept the *Gayl*'s engines off. They were almost home. Earth was less than a day away.

"Sam managed to dock us at the space station in one piece," Josh said happily. "Yippee! He's not totally useless after all!"

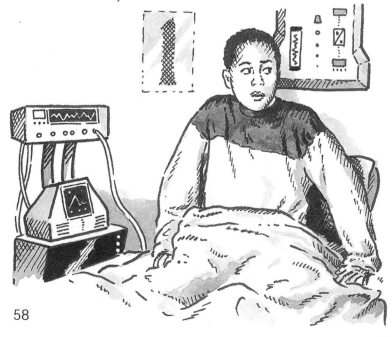

"Our tractor beam brought you in," the doctor said. "It was touch and go there for a while. We had no idea your ship was so badly damaged. We found you slumped over the control console. Your body stopped the autopilot from coming back on line."

Josh looked around the room again. Sam was nowhere to be seen.

"Where's Sam?" he asked. Suddenly he felt anxious. "Is he all right?"

"We have a problem with Sam," Dr Dalder said slowly. "We've watched your log transmission tapes a number of times ..."

"And?" Josh prompted. "Sam's in trouble, isn't he? I knew it! I knew that's why he couldn't tell me anything about himself." Josh glared at the doctor and General Collins. "Listen, if it wasn't for Sam, I wouldn't be here. He probably saved my life, What're you doing to him?"

Josh was already getting off the bed. Sam was his friend. He wasn't going to let them do anything to Sam without putting up a fight first.

"Josh, relax. We're not doing anything to Sam. I promise," General Collins soothed.

"Josh, the mind ... the mind is a very strange thing. Even now we still don't fully understand it," Dr Dalder began carefully.

"What are you talking about?" Josh frowned. What did this have to do with Sam?

"We know that the mind will close down to protect itself. In fact it will do whatever is necessary to survive," the doctor continued.

"What's all that got to do with anything?"

"Tell me this, Josh," Dr Dalder said. "How did you feel after your family and friends died?"

Josh lowered his gaze away from the doctor. He shrugged. "Scared ... I didn't know if I'd be the next to die or not. And lonely ..."

"And how did you feel just before Sam arrived on your ship?"

Josh didn't answer. He couldn't.

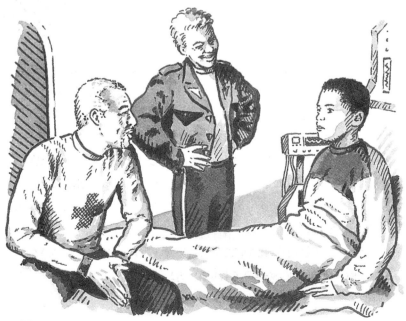

"Did you think about just giving up?" Dr Dalder asked. "About just going to bed and not coming out again?"

Still Josh said nothing.

"If you give me an honest answer, I suspect it may explain everything," the doctor said gently.

"I ... sometimes felt like that. Sometimes a lot," Josh admitted reluctantly.

"I think it was more than a lot. I think you were very close to giving up for good when your friend Sam came along," Dr Dalder said softly.

"I was on my own for almost two years. I thought I'd go crazy or worse and I didn't know if I'd ever see Earth again," Josh said, turning to look out of the portscreen again, "I still don't see what this has got to do with Sam. Where is he?"

"Josh, listen to me," Dr Dalder said earnestly. "There is no Sam. We've watched your logs and we can see no one but you on the tape. It looks to us as if you're talking to yourself. And according to the *Gayl*'s readouts, after the plague there was never anyone on the ship except you."

Josh stared at him. "This is some kind of joke, right?" he said, with a suspicious guffaw.

"No joke, Josh. I believe there was no Sam, except in your mind. He was conjured up by your brain to stop you feeling so isolated, so alone. In the logs you recorded, you yourself said he stopped you from going crazy."

"I don't understand ..." Josh stared at the doctor.

"It's quite simple," Dr Dalder smiled. "Sam was your loneliness cure. He was your brain's way of protecting you from the loneliness and isolation you felt. And now you're safe you don't need him anymore."

"He was all in my mind?" Josh struggled to realize what the doctor was telling him. "Does that mean I'm crazy?"

"Of course not. Sam was your way of stopping yourself from going crazy. He served his purpose." Dr Dalder smiled. "Once you get back to Earth, you'll make new friends in no time at all."

Josh turned back to look at the planet below him.

"Come on, General. I think Josh needs to be on his own for a while. He's got a lot to think about," Dr Dalder said.

Josh listened as the adults left his room. Was it true? Was Sam just in his mind – like an imaginary friend? Or maybe the doctor was wrong and Sam was real. Just because his image didn't show up on the transmission logs didn't mean that Sam didn't exist. Sam could have been a new alien life form that *couldn't* show up on the transmission tapes.

Josh smiled slowly. It didn't really matter what Sam was or wasn't. Sam was his friend – and Josh knew he'd never, ever forget him.

"Whoever you were and wherever you were from," Josh said quietly, "thank you."

THE END